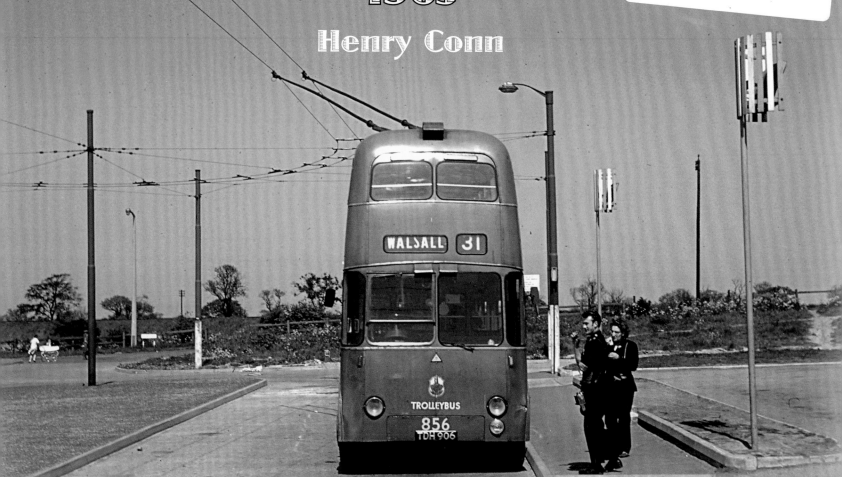

Buses, Trolleybuses & Recoll...
1963

Henry Conn

Contents

© Henry Conn 2017

First published in 2017

British Library Cataloguing in Publication Data

Title page **WALSALL** Service 31 was extended from Abbey Square on 20 September 1959 to a turning circle adjacent to the 'Eagle' public house close to the borough boundary at Broad Lane; the pub is off to the right of this view taken on 28 June 1963. The crew of No 856 (TDH 906), a Willowbrook-bodied Sunbeam F4A new in April 1955, will probably have a short break before returning to St Paul's Street bus station.

Acknowledgements

Most of the illustrations in this book are from the camera of Tony Belton, and without these wonderful views this book would not have been possible. My most sincere thanks to Tony – outstanding.

The PSV Circle Fleet Histories for the operators in this book and a number of issues of *Buses Illustrated* were vital sources of information.

A catalogue record for this book is available from the British Library.

ISBN 978 1 85794 512 6

Silver Link Publishing Ltd
The Trundle
Ringstead Road
Great Addington
Kettering
Northants NN14 4BW

Tel/Fax: 01536 330588
email: sales@nostalgiacollection.com
Website: www.nostalgiacollection.com

Printed and bound in the Czech Republic

Unless otherwise credited, all the pictures in this book were taken by Tony Belton

Introduction

Most years before and after 1963 have experienced a number of seminal moments, but a look at that particular year reminds us just how many significant events took place: Martin Luther King Jnr's famous 'I have a dream' speech, the assassination of President John F. Kennedy, and the beginning of 'Beatlemania' are just some of the history-altering events that made 1963 one of the most memorable years in world history.

Nelson Rockefeller began his second term as New York's Governor, and President Kennedy delivered his 1963 State of the Union speech in the year that he turned 46. In a televised press conference, he warned the Soviet Union that if offensive weapons were again found on Cuba, it would 'produce the greatest crisis the world has faced in its history'. Kennedy ordered military retaliation against any Cuban ship or plane attacking the US by sea or air, after two MIG jet fighters fired at an unarmed American shrimp boat in the Florida Straits. New York City had been without mass-circulation newspapers since a printers' strike on 9 December, and the US asked that all Russian troops be removed from Cuba. America froze all Cuban assets, some $33 million, and the Cuban Communist Government seized the US embassy in Havana, an action believed unprecedented in modern diplomacy. The building was the property of the US Government, and the move was in reprisal for the freezing of Cuban accounts.

The United States and the Soviet Union signed an agreement setting up a 'hot line' circuit to keep constant contact between Moscow and Washington and help prevent an accidental war. Meanwhile the Communist regime of East Germany created a wide forbidden zone on its side of the Berlin Wall and elsewhere to stop escapes and sever any remaining tenuous contact between Berliners. For 76 miles along the border with East Germany the banned zone was 545 yards wide, while along the concrete wall and barbed wire that snaked for 25 miles across Berlin itself it was 109 yards wide.

President Kennedy opened his tour of Europe with an enormous welcome from almost a million West Germans in Cologne, Bonn and the Rhineland countryside. At one point during the day he shouted 'Ich bin ein Berliner' ('I am a Berliner') and was silenced by thunderous applause. The President then visited the Berlin Wall.

Despite this, a Berlin-bound convoy of US Army infantrymen was held up at a Soviet checkpoint, and when it tried to break through it was checked by Soviet armoured vehicles. American military forces in West Germany were alerted for possible military action, but 41 hours later, and for no apparent reason, the Soviet Union gave in and let the convoy through.

On 8 August a son was born prematurely to the Kennedys. He was said to weigh only 4lb 10½oz and was born by Caesarean section. Sadly he was diagnosed with idiopathic respiratory distress syndrome and was placed in an incubator-type device, the only one of its kind in the world, but died shortly afterwards.

On 22 November in Dallas, while riding in a motorcade with Texas Governor John Connally, President Kennedy was shot. Never regaining consciousness, he died on the operating table at 1.00pm. The suspect, Lee Harvey Oswald, was caught in a darkened movie theatre in the Oak Cliff area of the city, about a mile and a half from the assassination. Earlier Police Officer J. D. Tippit had also been shot and killed by Oswald near the same theatre. Governor Connally, who was riding in a jump seat directly in front of the President, was shot in the chest, but after a four-hour operation

he was reported to be in a satisfactory condition. Oswald was subsequently shot and killed in Dallas police headquarters by local nightclub owner Jack Ruby. Ruby stepped up, unnoticed by either Oswald or the detective beside him, and fired a single shot, point blank, into Oswald's stomach. Oswald grabbed his stomach, grunted in agony and pitched over onto the concrete floor; he died 1¾ hours later. An estimated 800,000 people lined the streets to pay their respects as the President's body was brought from the Capitol to the White House. Three acres of Arlington National Cemetery surrounding his grave were set aside as a memorial to him.

Alcatraz Federal Prison was closed for good and there are no specific plans for its future. The Government decided on closure after discovering that it would cost millions for repairs and upgrades. Because it was accessible only by water, Alcatraz was the most expensive prison to maintain. Also this year Robert Stroud, 'The Birdman of Alcatraz', died, having won fame when he made a study of bird diseases at the federal pen at Leavenworth.

The US and Britain sign an agreement whereby American Polaris missiles would be sold to the United Kingdom for use in British submarines. At a White House ceremony President Kennedy proclaimed Sir Winston Churchill an honorary citizen of the United States, an accolade never before bestowed upon a citizen of another nation. Churchill later announced that he was suffering from greatly reduced mobility due to a hip injury the previous year and was retiring from political life, ending a long career. Also in 1963 Diana Churchill, his eldest daughter, ended her life with a sleeping pill overdose.

The US atomic submarine Thresher, carrying a crew of 129, vanished after a steep test dive in the Atlantic. Freshman Senator Edward M. Kennedy, youngest brother of the President, gave his first interview as a senator. Astronaut Gordon Cooper overcame a suspenseful electrical equipment failure

in his Mercury Faith 7 spacecraft and headed for earth for a pinpoint landing; he had completed 22 orbits of the Earth during America's longest manned space flight. Project Mercury then officially ended, and NASA announced that there would be no more Americans orbiting the earth for at least another year and probably longer.

Elsewhere in America, a gas explosion ripped through the Indianapolis Coliseum during a 'Holiday on Ice' performance, leaving 64 either dead or dying and hundreds injured, and Frank Sinatra Jnr was kidnapped at gunpoint from his motel in Stateline, Nevada.

Dr Martin Luther King Jnr was released from jail in Birmingham, Alabama, and almost 125,000 people took part in a massive demonstration as he led a massive 'walk to freedom' through downtown Detroit. In another 'March for Freedom', more than 200,000 blacks and white sympathisers massed before the Lincoln Memorial in Washington, demanding across-the-board abolition of race discrimination.

Pope John XXIII, who had presided over the world's half a billion Roman Catholics for more than four years, died from peritonitis and Pope Paul VI succeeded him.

In Britain the Great Train Robbery took place at Cheddington in Buckinghamshire; three men and two women were subsequently arrested. The gang escaped with £2.5 million in currency, a large part of which was recovered.

Harold Macmillan resigned as Prime Minister and nominated Foreign Secretary Lord Home to succeed him, and Labour Party leader Hugh Gaitskell died and Harold Wilson was elected leader. The steam locomotive Flying Scotsman made its last scheduled run, and the Beatles recorded Please Please Me in a single session. The Bond film Dr No was released in the USA, and the second in the series, From Russia with Love, opened in London.

On 20 November 1962, unremarkably, light snow had fallen, and during the first days of December temperatures fell to below freezing. On the afternoon of Boxing Day, however, heavy snowfall began, and on 29 December the country was covered by blizzards, with snow blanketing the whole of the UK until the end of January 1963, lying thick in many areas until March. The weather began to affect the economy with rising food prices, and throughout February there was heavy snow and storms, and a 36-hour blizzard caused drifts of 20 feet in some areas. On 1 March the temperatures exceeded freezing for the first time since November, and by the 5th the last traces of the Boxing Day snow had vanished. Three days later it rained – a winter never to be forgotten.

Enjoy the nostalgia…

Scotland

SCOURIE, HIGHLAND Exchanging mail at Scourie on 12 December is Sutherland Transport and Trading Commer FJS 685, which will return to Kinlochbervie; I think the other bus is Bedford NS 4745, which was based in Scourie at the time this view was taken. The Ford Cortina Estate is relatively new, as the first estate model left the production lines in March 1963. *Author's collection*

On this day Kenya gained independence from the UK.

ABERDEEN A warm day in the 'Granite City'! The upper-deck sliding vents of No 51 (DRG 451), a Weymann-bodied AEC Regent III new in June 1949, are open and the gentleman walking past is in short sleeves. It is 1 July and No 51 still retains the grey roof livery that was phased out by 1964; the bus would be withdrawn in 1967 and transferred to the Corporation Works Department. *Author's collection*

Left: **ABERDEEN** Between December 1946 and June 1947 Aberdeen Corporation purchased new 15 'RT'-type Weymann-bodied AEC Regent IIIs, Nos 17 to 31 (BRS 517 to 531). This is No 23 (BRS 523) working service 9 between Garden City and Byron Square on 10 October; it be withdrawn and sold for scrap in 1965. *Author's collection*

The second James Bond movie, From Russia with Love, opened in the UK on this day.

Right: **DUNDEE** Corporation took delivery of 10 Barnard-bodied Daimler CVD6s in 1949, and all received new Alexander H33/28R bodies between 1959 and 1960. Representing this rebodied batch on 8 August, working service 2, is No 121 (ATS 901). This bus became a driver trainer, T1, in 1975 and passed to Tayside Regional Council on 16 May of that year. *Author's collection*

The Great Train Robbery had taken place in Buckinghamshire during the early hours.

Left: **LOCATION UNKNOWN** A unique bus was SB 7600, a Willenhall-bodied Morris new to McLachlan in 1950. Willenhall Coachcraft was established as a car body repair garage at the County Bridge Works in Willenhall, Staffordshire, in the 1930s and during the boom years of the late 1940s a portion of the works was turned over to coach bodies. *Author's collection*

Above: **HADDINGTON** New to Fairbairn of Haddington was SS 7501, a Duple-bodied Bedford OB with a Perkins P6 diesel engine new in 1949. Having been acquired by Ian Glass, this view of the bus was taken on 23 November, indicating a journey to Garvald, a small village south-east of Haddington. *Author's collection*

On this day, 23 November, the first episode of Doctor Who was broadcast on the BBC.

Above right: **GLASGOW** Arriving in Buchanan Street on 8 April is SMT No AA2 (NSG 779), an ECW-bodied Bristol LD6G new in January 1956. It was one of a batch of 15, the first to be delivered to SMT, and would be withdrawn and exported to the USA in August 1976. *Author's collection*

On this day the film Lawrence of Arabia won the Best Picture award at the 35th Academy Awards at Santa Monica Civic Auditorium.

Right: **BARRHEAD** Standing at McGill's depot on 5 December are, from the left, GVD 47, a Duple-bodied Guy Arab that had been new to Hutchison of Overtown in 1952, CHS 355, a Guy Arab new in 1945 and rebodied by Massey in 1955, and JXC 201, a Cravens-bodied AEC Regent III new to London Transport in 1949 and acquired by McGill's from Garelochhead Coach services in 1960. *Author's collection*

Skier Eddie Edwards, 'Eddie the Eagle', was born on this day in Cheltenham.

Below: **CASTLE DOUGLAS** Taking a break from buses, the railway station is seen here on 5 June. The steam locomotive is British Railways 2-6-4T No 80052, completed at Brighton Works on 5 December 1952 and working from Corkerhill depot in Pollokshaws, Glasgow, when this view was taken. No 80052 was withdrawn from service on 7 July 1964 and had been broken up at the Inslow Works of Motherwell Machinery & Scrap in Wishaw by 31 March 1965. *Author's collection*

Above: **ROTHESAY** On a wet and miserable 22 March, Western SMT No 1269 (JSD 905), an Alexander coach-bodied Bristol LS6G new in 1957, is picking up passengers outside the Bute Arms Hotel for the journey to Port Bannatyne. The Bute Arms was gutted by fire in the summer of 1982. *Author's collection*

On this day The Beatles released their first album, Please Please Me.

Above right: **ROTHESAY** Working a local service on the same day is No 341 (BCS 302), an all-Leyland PD1 new in 1947. Just behind it is No 340 (BCS 301), another vehicle from the same batch. *Author's collection*

CASTLE DOUGLAS No 80052 has just left Castle Douglas station and is passing No 2 signal box, about to take the branch line to Kirkcudbright. *Author's collection*

On this day John Profumo was forced to admit that he lied to the House of Commons, an unforgivable offence in British politics, about his affair with Christine Keeler. He resigned from office, from the House, and from the Privy Council. Before making his public confession, Profumo confessed the affair to his wife, who stood by him. It was never shown that his relationship with Keeler had led to any breach of national security, but the scandal rocked the Conservative Government and was generally held to have been among the causes of its defeat by Labour at the 1964 General Election.

Photo	DESTINATIONS
14	NEWCASTLE UPON TYNE
15	NEWCASTLE UPON TYNE
16	NEWCASTLE UPON TYNE
17	SOUTH SHIELDS
18	SOUTH SHIELDS
19	SOUTH SHIELDS
20	SOUTH SHIELDS
21	SOUTH SHIELDS
22	MIDDLESBROUGH
23	MIDDLESBROUGH
24	HULL
25	HULL
26	HULL
27	HULL

Tyneside and Teesside

Right inset: **NEWCASTLE-UPON-TYNE** The same trolleybus is seen again on the same day. Route 34 would cease trolleybus operations on 1 June, and No 488 would be withdrawn and sold for scrap in July 1965.

Right: **NEWCASTLE-UPON-TYNE** trolleybus route 34 was the first of the city's routes to go. The reason given at the time by the Corporation was that extensive road works planned at Pilgrim Street on the north side of the Tyne Bridge would make it too difficult and expensive to reroute the wiring, and buses would be more adaptable to the changes in the road network. This is MCCW-bodied BUT 9641T No 488 (LTN 488), new in April 1948, on route 34 on 14 April.

NEWCASTLE-UPON-TYNE Working a 34A service, also on 14 April, is No 523 (LTN 523), an NCB-bodied Sunbeam S7 new in December 1948; it was withdrawn and, like No 488, sold for scrap in July 1965. The United bus heading into town is an ECW-bodied Bristol K.

Right: **SOUTH SHIELDS** Working on route 4 to the suburb of Chichester on Bank Holiday Monday, 15 April, is South Shields No 254 (CU 4876), an NCB-bodied Karrier W4 new in August 1947; it was withdrawn and sold for scrap in March 1964.

On this day more than 70,000 marchers arrived in London from Aldermaston to demonstrate against nuclear weapons.

Below: **SOUTH SHIELDS** Climbing up to Marsden Inn on the same day, with the seafront in the background, is No 267 (CU 5279), an NCB-bodied Sunbeam F4 that was new in August 1950 and sold for scrap in August 1964.

On this day the White House announced that the First Lady, Jackie Kennedy was pregnant.

Below: **SOUTH SHIELDS** With the 'Adam and Eve' public house on Frederick Street in the background, No 270 (CU 5282), another NCB-bodied Sunbeam F4, heads for Westoe, also on 15 April. Note in the right background that there are three policemen by the traffic lights – was there trouble in the pub?

Right: **SOUTH SHIELDS** Leaving the Marsden Inn turning circle the same day is No 246 (CU 4716), an NCB-bodied Karrier W4 new in January 1947 with bodywork built to relaxed utility specifications. This trolleybus would be withdrawn and scrapped within a few days.

Below: **SOUTH SHIELDS** Very few trolleybuses were bodied by East Lancashire (Bridlington) Limited, but St Helens Corporation took delivery of eight between December 1950 and February 1951. All eight were acquired by South Shields in July 1958, and this is No 206 (BDJ 78) at Marsden Inn; it entered service in 1959 and was withdrawn and sold for scrap in April 1963.

Above: **MIDDLESBROUGH** Between May and July 1950 Teesside Railless Traction Board took delivery of seven East Lancashire (Bridlington)-bodied Sunbeam F4s, Nos 1 to 7 (GAJ 11 to 17). At Normanby terminus, on the outskirts of Middlesbrough, on Bank Holiday Monday 15 April is No 2 (GAJ 12). This trolleybus received a new Roe body in September 1964 and, after withdrawal in April 1971, passed into preservation.

MIDDLESBROUGH Passing under the low railway bridge in Bolckow Road in Grangetown, Middlesbrough, is No 6 (GAJ 16), another of the same batch of Sunbeam F4s.

The No 1 single on this Bank Holiday was How Do You Do It? *by Gerry and the Pacemakers.*

Hull

HULL All the following Hull views were taken on 13 June. In the first we see trolleybus No 110 (RKH 110), a Roe-bodied Sunbeam MF2B new in January 1955, turning at the Endike terminus of route 63. No 110 was withdrawn after the last day of trolleybus operations in Hull on 31 October 1964.

The day before this view was taken the long-awaited film Cleopatra had its premiere in New York.

1963
No 1 Records

January
Bachelor Boy   *Cliff Richard*
Dance on   *Shadows*
Diamonds   *Jet Harris & Tony Meehan*
February
Wayward Wind   *Frank Ifield*
March
Summer Holiday   *Cliff Richard*
Foot tapper   *Shadows*
April
How do you do it?   *Gerry & The Pacemakers*
May
From me to you   *Beatles*
June
I like it   *Gerry & The Pacemakers*
July
Confessing that I love you   *Frank Ifield*
August
Devil in disguise   *Elvis Presley*
Sweets for my sweet   *Searchers*
Bad to me   *Billy J. Kramer & The Dakotas*
September
She loves you   *Beatles*
October
Do you love me? *Brian Poole & The Tremeloes*
November
You'll never walk alone   *Gerry & The*
                                  Pacemakers
December
I want to hold your hand   *Beatles*

HULL In my opinion, probably one of the best-looking trolleybuses to enter service in the UK was the Roe-bodied Sunbeam MF2B as operated by Hull Corporation. No 110 is seen again heading for Beverley Road on the 63 service in a remarkably quiet King Edward Street.

The No 1 single on this day was From Me To You by the Beatles.

Below: **HULL** Taken from an unusual vantage point, and approaching Stepney level crossing on Beverley Road, is another Roe-bodied Sunbeam MF2B, No 111 (RKH 111), new in January 1955.

Above: **HULL** No 111 is captured nicely again by the photographer in King Edward Street. This view shows the dual-entrance/exit Roe bodywork and the prompt to the travelling public showing where the entrance is. I also like the route number and destination on the side of the trolleybus.

The album Please Please Me *by the Beatles was the No 1 album from May for 30 weeks.*

Doncaster, Bradford and Huddersfield

Right: **DONCASTER** These Doncaster views were all taken on 4 April. During 1962 and 1963 Doncaster Corporation transferred used Roe bodywork from trolleybuses to 12 new Daimler CVG6 chassis. All the bodies were converted from full-front to half-cab type, and representing this transfer and redesign of bodywork is No 172 (172 GDT). The trolleybus in Beckett Road is No 369 (CDT 312), a Roe rebodied Karrier new in 1943 and sold for scrap in late 1963.

Right: **DONCASTER** With Clock Corner in view, we see No 373 (CDT 625), a Karrier new in 1945; it received a new Roe body in 1954 and remained in the fleet until closure of the trolleybus system in Doncaster on 14 December 1963. On the right after Burtons is the 'Elephant', which opened in 1915 and was demolished in the mid-1970s.

DONCASTER No 373 is seen again heading for the Race Course, closely followed by No 166 (4166 DT), a Roe-bodied AEC Regent V new in 1960. This bus was sold in July 1970 and acquired by Parsons of St Albans in September of that year.

DONCASTER Standing opposite the 'Elephant' is No 375 (CDT 636); new in 1945, it received a new Roe body in 1955, and made the final journeys of the Doncaster trolleybus system on the evening of 14 December 1963. Passing the trolleybus is No 167 (4167 DT) a Roe-bodied AEC Regent V new in 1960; it would be sold for further service with Anderton of Birmingham from July 1970 until September 1971.

DONCASTER The Harry Jacobs neon sign stands out in this wintry April scene. On route 6 to the Race Course is No 375 once more.

BRADFORD During April 1953 Bradford Corporation acquired 17 AEC 661Ts and 15 BUT 9611Ts, all bodied by Weymann, from the Nottinghamshire and Derbyshire fleet. Turning at Saltaire on 20 February is No 593 (HNU 971), one of the AECs, which entered service with Bradford in August 1954; it received a new East Lancashire body in January 1958 and remained in the fleet until withdrawal in 1965.

Left: **BRADFORD** At
Duckworth Lane terminus
on 21 February is a freshly
repainted No 726 (DKY 726),
a Karrier W new in February
1946; it received a new East
Lancashire body in June 1959
and was sold for scrap in
August 1971.

*The No 1 single at this time
was Frank Ifield's* Wayward
Wind.

Right: **BRADFORD**
Departing from the
Duckworth Lane terminus
on the same day, with the
Bradford Royal Infirmary on
the right, is No 733 (DKY
733), a Karrier W that was
new in May 1946; it received
its new East Lancashire body
in June 1959 and was sold
for scrap in March 1973.
Bradford Royal Infirmary was
built in 1936 and is at present
a large teaching hospital.

BRADFORD Standing on the forecourt of Saltaire depot on 20 February is No 743 (EKU 743), a Roe-bodied BUT 9611T that was new in December 1949 and became a tuition vehicle in December 1966. It was withdrawn in December 1970 and acquired by the National Trolleybus Association for preservation in November 1972.

Right: **BRADFORD** Negotiating the Saltaire terminus on the same day is No 757 (FKU 757), a Weymann-bodied BUT 9611T. New in January 1951, it was sold for scrap in August 1971. The two-tone van behind it is a Ford Thames 309E; in March 1965 the Thames name was discontinued and from then on they were called Ford Anglia vans.

Below: **BRADFORD** Passing Thornbury depot on 21 February is No 811 (BDY 801), one of 12 Sunbeam Ws acquired from Maidstone & District (original Hastings Tramway Co) between June and August 1959. Carrying a Park Royal body, it was new in February 1946 and sold for scrap in April 1964.

Below right: **BRADFORD** acquired six East Lancashire-bodied BUT 9611Ts from Darlington Corporation in February 1960, registered LHN 780 to 785); they had been new to Darlington in April and May 1949. Five of them received new East Lancashire bodies in June and July 1962, but LHN 780 was not operated and was dismantled for spares. At Saltaire roundabout on 20 February is No 831 (LHN 781), which was sold for scrap in March 1973.

BRADFORD Turning at Bingley terminus on that same February day is No 832 (LHN 782), another of the East Lancashire-bodied former Darlington BUT 9611Ts.

Cliff Richard and the Shadows were top of the album charts with Summer Holiday.

Left: **BRADFORD** No 832 has completed the turn at Bingley terminus and the crew are about to change the destination indicators.

Below left: **BRADFORD** As chassis only, Bradford acquired 12 Sunbeam F4s from Mexborough & Swinton in April 1961; seven received new East Lancashire bodies and the remaining five chassis were dismantled for spares. This is No 844 (FWX 914), which entered service after rebodying in December 1962. This vehicle had the distinction of being the last trolleybus in service in Bradford.

Below: **HUDDERSFIELD** Opened on 1 September 1939, the Longwood trolleybus turntable was used to turn all Huddersfield trolleybuses terminating at Dod-Lea, where there was insufficient space for them to reverse direction under their own power. Arriving at Longwood on 21 February is No 569 (ECS 169), a Sunbeam MS2 that was new on 1 January 1949 with a Park Royal body. It received a new Roe body and re-entered service on 24 March 1958, then was sold for scrap on 6 February 1964, a little under a year after this view was taken.

HUDDERSFIELD Manually operated, the turntable only remained in use until 1940, when wartime conditions led to the recruitment of female conductresses who were not strong enough to help the driver operate it. Also, blackout regulations made it difficult for the crew to see what they were doing after dark. The turntable was therefore replaced by alternative arrangements, and was not put back into service after the end of the war. This view, taken just a few minutes after the previous one, shows No 569 reversing onto the turntable.

HUDDERSFIELD The Longwood turntable is said to have been one of only four trolleybus turntables constructed worldwide. The awkward reversal onto the turntable is highlighted in this view taken on the same day of No 622 (KVH 222), an East Lancashire-bodied BUT 9641T that entered service on 12 October 1956 and was sold for scrap on 2 July 1968.

Manchester

MANCHESTER All the following views of Manchester and Ashton trolleybuses were taken on 28 August. The Manchester Corporation Ashton New Road trolleybus services started on 31 July 1938 as routes 26 and 27. They were renumbered 215, Stevenson Square to Audenshaw and Stevenson Square to Stalybridge, on 17 April 1950. Just departing from Hyde Road depot, and indicating a short working 215X, which should be to Clayton North Lane and Edge Lane, is No 1310 (ONE 710), a BUT 9612T with Burlingham bodywork, built at the Crossley factory and new in 1955. Behind, working a service 109X, is No 3578 (UNB 578), an MCCW-bodied Leyland PD2/40 new in 1959.

Right: **MANCHESTER** Passing Hyde Park depot working a service 216X is No 1316 (ONE 716), a Burlingham-bodied BUT 9612T new in 1955. Alongside, working a Limited Stop 33X, is No 2050 (GVR 144), an all-Crossley DD42/4 that was new in 1948 and was sold for scrap in 1965.

Far right: **MANCHESTER** Running alongside the railway arches in Waterloo Road, working service 216, is No 1320 (ONE 720) from the same batch. It would survive until the end of the Manchester system on 30 December 1966.

Right: **MANCHESTER** About to exit Hyde Park depot is Burlingham-bodied BUT 9641T No 1331 (ONE 731).

On this day, 28 August, the Rev Martin Luther King Jnr delivered his 'I have a dream' speech on the steps of the Lincoln Memorial to an audience estimated to have been at least 250,000 strong.

MANCHESTER Passing Hyde Park depot working a 212X short working is No 1357 (ONE 757), a Burlingham-bodied BUT9612T new in 1956. Also to be seen is the angular rear end of a Triumph Herald, while the van on the left is a Ford Thames 300E, which was produced between 1954 and 1961.

Right: **MANCHESTER** The 29 trolleybus route ran to Guide Bridge from 16 October 1939 and was extended to Ashton on 22 March 1940. From 17 April 1950 the service was renumbered 219 and originally had a clockwise terminal loop in the city, but the terminus was moved to Portman Street on 16 June 1957. The 219 was jointly worked by Manchester and Ashton and was withdrawn without ceremony on 10 October 1964, replaced by buses. Leaving Portman Street for Ashton is No 1361 (ONE 761), numerically the second-last Burlingham-bodied BUT 9612T new in 1956; on the right is No 1308 (ONE 708), another of the Burlingham-bodied BUT 9612Ts, this time from 1955.

Top far right: **ASHTON** At Ashton's Market Hall on a joint working of route 218 is Ashton Corporation No 83 (YTE 822), a Bond-bodied BUT 9612T new in October 1956. It survived until the closure of the Manchester/Ashton trolleybus system in December 1966 and was sold for scrap in February the following year.

Right: **ASHTON** This lovely view of Ashton No 86 (YTE 825), a Bond-bodied BUT 9641 new in 1956, was taken on the same day.

On this day the Beatles were interviewed in Manchester. The discussion was filmed by BBC Television and used as part of a documentary entitled The Mersey Sound.

Wolverhampton and Walsall

WOLVERHAMPTON In 1931 the last phase of trolleybus expansion in Wolverhampton began when the interwar housing estates were served by trolleybuses, and one of these was the conversion of the Penn route from buses to trolleybuses. On 9 June 1963 the last trolleybuses ran to Penn and Penn Fields, and on that day No 414 (DUK 14), a Sunbeam W4 new in 1945 and rebodied by Park Royal in 1952, is seen in Broad Street passing the de-wired No 435 (EJW 435), a Sunbeam W4 new in 1948 and rebodied by Roe in 1961. No 414 was withdrawn after the closure of the Penn route, but No 435 remained until 1967.

On this day Jim Clark won the Belgian Grand Prix at Spa.

WOLVERHAMPTON This is the St James's Square terminus, which was a loop on the southern side of Horseley Fields. Waiting for a driver to take up the journey on a service 5 to Willenhall on 28 July is No 432 (DUK 832), which was new in 1946 and rebodied by Roe in 1959, remaining in the fleet until 1967. To the left is No 550 (FJW 550), a Park Royal-bodied Guy Arab III new in 1950.

1963 Happenings (1)

January
England suffers the coldest winter since 1740.
The hit film *Summer Holiday* starring Cliff Richard is released.
Hugh Gaitskell, leader of the Labour Party, dies.
General De Gaulle vetoes UK entry into the Common Market (EEC).

February
Harold Wilson becomes leader of the Labour Party.

March
Publication of the infamous 'Beeching Report' on the future of British Railways.

April
Princess Alexandra marries Angus Ogilvy at Westminster Abbey.

June
Pope John XXIII dies, Pope Paul VI instituted.
John Profumo, Secretary of State for War, resigns over affair with Christine Keeler.

August
UK, US and Russia sign a partial nuclear test ban treaty in Moscow.
'Great Train Robbery'; £2.5 million stolen from a Glasgow – London mail train in Buckinghamshire.
Dr Martin Luther King makes 'I have a dream' speech in Washington.

Below: **WOLVERHAMPTON** Passing the Midland Counties Dairy at the junction of Lea Road and Penn Road, also on 9 June, is No 621 (FJW 621), a Park Royal-bodied Sunbeam F4 new in 1949 and withdrawn in 1964. Behind the trolleybus on route 46 is No 42 (4042 JW), a Metro-Cammell-bodied Guy Arab IV new in 1960. I think the Midland Counties Dairy building is now a drive-through McDonalds!

On this day Johnny Depp was born in Owensboro, Kentucky.

Right: **WOLVERHAMPTON** Picking up passengers on route 11 at the junction of Thornley Street and Broad Street on that last day is No 626 (FJW 626), a Park Royal-bodied Sunbeam F4 new in 1950 and withdrawn in 1965.

Above: **WALSALL** The loading stop for Wolverhampton after 1950 was the north side of the cinema in Townend Street. This quiet view of No 638 (FJW 638), a Park Royal-bodied Guy BT new in 1949, was taken on 28 July. Entering Townend Street is Walsall trolleybus No 309 (BDY 816), a Weymann-bodied Sunbeam W4 that had been new to Hastings Tramways in June 1948 and was acquired by Walsall in June 1959, entering service in October. In the 1960s the former Hastings trolleybuses were common performers on route 29.

Left: **WOLVERHAMPTON** On Penn Road at its junction with Goldthorn Hill is No 635 (FJW 635), a Park Royal-bodied Guy BT new in 1949 and withdrawn in 1964. The Bedford trailer unit loaded with empty milk bottles is presumably on its way to the Midland Counties Dairy.

1963 Happenings (2)

September
> Christine Keeler arrested for perjury; Denning Report on Profumo Affair published. Fylingdales early warning station comes into operation.

October
> Harold Macmillan resigns as Prime Minister and is succeeded by Sir Alec Douglas-Home.

November
> Dartford Tunnel opens.
> US President John F. Kennedy assassinated; Lyndon B. Johnson becomes US President.

December
> Greek liner *Lakonia* sinks 250 miles west of Gibralter while on a Christmas cruise.

1963 TV Favourites: a selection (1)

World in Action
This hard-hitting current affairs programme was first seen in January 1963, and tackled many controversial topics in succeeding years.

Ready, Steady, Go!
Almost compulsory Friday evening viewing for teenagers, this show proclaimed 'The weekend starts here!'

Far left: **WOLVERHAMPTON**
This view was taken at Wolverhampton's Park Lane depot on 10 June, and all three trolleybuses in view have just been withdrawn from service, never to run again. They are Park Royal-bodied Sunbeam W4s Nos 470 and 463, both new in 1948, flanking No 402, new in 1944 and rebodied by Park Royal in 1952.

Above: **WOLVERHAMPTON** A few moments later No 404 (DJW 904), a Park Royal-rebodied Sunbeam W4 new in 1944, is being shunted to go alongside No 463 as withdrawn from service.

On this day US President Kennedy chose to announce his decision to suspend nuclear testing and work towards a nuclear test-ban treaty with the other atomic powers.

Left: **WOLVERHAMPTON** The overhead wires are in a need of repair as No 486 (FJW 486), a Park Royal-bodied Guy BT, awaits its turn to be parked up and withdrawn. In the background on the right is No 565 (FJW 565), an all-Guy Arab III new in 1949 and seen here awaiting the scrapman.

Right: **WALSALL** Turning from Green Lane into Townend Street on 29 June is Walsall's No 304 (BDY 808), a Weymann-bodied Sunbeam W4. New to Hastings Tramways in September 1947, the trolleybus was acquired by Walsall in July 1959 and entered service in November. The wiring was changed in 1967 to permit trolleybuses on service 33 to enter Townend Street from the left of this view rather than from the right as seen here.

Above: **WALSALL** At St James Square on 30 June, No 305 (BDY 811), another of the Weymann-bodied Sunbeam W4s, is overtaking No 640 (FJW 640), a Park Royal-bodied Guy BT new in 1949 and shortly to be withdrawn from service. No 305 would be withdrawn in November 1965 and sold for scrap in August 1967. St James Square had been used as a terminus for joint service 29 from 15 October 1951.

Above right: **WALSALL** Departing from St Paul's Street bus station and entering St Paul's Street on the same day is No 334 (NDH 951), a Brush-bodied Sunbeam F4. This trolleybus was exhibited at the 1950 Commercial Motor Show and entered service on 19 December of that year. It was withdrawn in late 1964 and languished for well over two years before being sold for scrap in August 1967.

Right: **WALSALL** Trolleybus services were extended beyond Bloxwich from 1955 with the opening of the wiring to Blakenall. This created a circular service numbered 30 clockwise and 15 anti-clockwise. Seen from the upper saloon of a trolleybus on 28 July, working service 30 on High Street, Leamore, with Field Road in the background, is No 854 (TDH 904), a Willowbrook-bodied Sunbeam F4A new in March 1955 and sold for scrap in November 1970.

Right: **WALSALL** On Sneyd Road at its junction with Mossley Lane and Sneyd Hall Road, working service 31 to Mossley Estate, is No 856 (TDH 906), a Willowbrook-bodied Sunbeam new in April 1955. The wiring off to the right was for service 33 via Dudley's Field Estate. Nos 856 and 871 were the first Walsall trolleybuses to be withdrawn from service on 31 March 1970; all the other Sunbeam F4As lasted until the system closed in October 1970.

Far right: **WALSALL** took delivery of its last new trolleybuses between June and October 1956; the seven vehicles were numbered 866 to 872 (XDH 66 to 72), and were Willowbrook-bodied Sunbeam F4As. This is No 872 at Townend Bank on 30 June in a view taken before the one-way system and the diversion of route 33 to the former 29 terminus in Townend Street. No 872 was Walsall's last trolleybus in service and is now preserved.

Right: **WALSALL** At 'The Eagle' terminus of route 31 on 29 June is No 874 (GFU 692). This trolleybus, a Northern Coachbuilders-bodied BUT 9611T, was new in July 1950 and was one of six acquired from Grimsby-Cleethorpes in July 1960. It entered service in Walsall in February 1962, was withdrawn in February 1970 and passed into preservation.

Above: **WALSALL** At Beechdale Estate terminus on the same day is another of the seven trolleybuses acquired from Grimsby-Cleethorpes. By comparison with No 874 in the previous view, No 877 (GFU 695) was extensively rebuilt before entering service on 15 January 1962, being lengthened to 30 feet and given a new front entrance. It survived to the end of the system in October 1970 and was sold for scrap a month later.

Above right: **WALSALL** Arriving in the town centre at Townend Bank on 29 June working a 33 is 877 which has arrived via Green Lane to the left of Richmond's semi-circular shop. Behind 877 is Stafford Street with wires leading to Birchills, Leamore and Bloxwich.

Right: **WALSALL** Departing from Blakenall terminus on 28 August working service 15 is No 862 (TDH 912), a Willowbrook-bodied Sunbeam F4A new in June 1955. On the left sister trolleybus No 864 (TDH 914) is on the stand. Both of these vehicles featured in the last trolleybus procession on 3 October 1970, and both were acquired for preservation.

Right: **WALSALL** The outer stand, Platform 4, at St Paul's Street bus station accommodated all the Walsall trolleybus services apart from those to Blakenall, which used the inner stand. No 864 is seen again leaving Platform 4 on 30 June outward-bound on service 30.

Below: **WALSALL** Inbound on service 33 on Green Lane near Rayboulds Bridge on the same day is Willowbrook-bodied Sunbeam F4A No 865 (TDH 915); the photograph was taken from the upper saloon of No 877.

1963 TV Favourites: a selection (2)

Doctor. Who
It was during the early evening of Saturday 23 November 1963 that we watched the first ever episode of *Doctor Who*, then played by William Hartnell. The Time Lord's ability to regenerate into various human forms has led to a number of actors playing the part over the years; the latest at the time of writing will be the first female Doctor being, Jodie Whittaker in the 2017/18 series.

Younger children enjoyed...
Boss Cat, Deputy Dawg and Fireball XL5.

The Dickie Henderson Show was one of the most popular comedy series of 1963.

Our Man at St Mark's was a gentle ecclesiastical comedy, starring Leslie Phillips as a young vicar.

The Marriage Lines starred Richard Briers and Prunella Scales as a newly wed young couple.

Above: **WALSALL** With its destination display ready for the inbound run to Walsall, this is No 866 (XDH 66), a Willowbrook-bodied Sunbeam F4A new in August 1956, at Beechdale Estate terminus, also on 30 June. In June 1969 No 866 was rebuilt with a forward entrance, making it suitable for one-person operation; it was also the last service trolleybus on 2 October 1970, but unfortunately did not escape the scrapman a month later.

Above right: **WALSALL** At the Townend Street terminus of the joint service 29 on 22 September is No 354 (ADX 192), a Park Royal-bodied Sunbeam F4 that had been new to Ipswich in July 1950 and was acquired by Walsall in May 1962. It entered service on 15 May 1963 but was involved in an accident on 26 May 1965 and withdrawn. When trolleybuses cease to operate on service 29 on 31 October 1965, following modification to the wiring, the loop became the Walsall terminus of service 33.

On this day the Beatles' She Loves You *was the No 1 single.*

Right: **DUDLEY** This is the Dudley terminus in Stone Street on 22 September, and on the right is Walsall's No 869 (XDH 69) on the Black Country Trolleybus tour, standing beside the long shelter at Dudley to accommodate passengers from Dudley Castle and Zoo. On the left, working route 58, is Wolverhampton's No 499 (FJW 499), a Park Royal-bodied Guy BT new in 1949.

Left: **WALSALL** From 31 December 1962 wires were extended from Bloxwich eastwards to a new housing estate at Lower Farm, and this would be the second-last extension of the Walsall system. Leaving St Paul's Street bus station on 29 June is No 870 (XDH 70), a Willowbrook-bodied Sunbeam F4A new in October 1956. At the time this view was taken the trolleybus fleet numbered 61 vehicles, with 60 operational and one rebuild to be completed. Following the last extension to the system, a half-mile branch off the Beechdale route to Cavendish Road on route 33, the route mileage was 19 miles.

Derby and Nottingham

Right: **DERBY** These photographs of Derby trolleybuses were taken on 7 August. Standing on the north side of the Market Place is No 172 (RC 8472), a Weymann-bodied Sunbeam W new in August 1944. A little over eight months later the trolleybus was sold into preservation.

Two days after this view was taken Whitney Houston – sadly no longer with us – was born in Newark, New Jersey.

Below left: **DERBY** Taken from the top saloon of another trolleybus, this is No 171 (RC 8471), a Weymann-bodied Sunbeam W new in July 1944, passing Alexandra Street on Osmaston Road while working a workers' special to Nightingale Road, which served the Rolls-Royce factory.

Right: **DERBY** Between December 1948 and March 1949 Derby took delivery of 30 Brush-bodied Sunbeam F4s, Nos 186 to 215 (ARC 486 to 515). This is No 206 (ARC 506) at the Douglas Street and Osmaston Road junction; it is indicating '02', which applied to depot-only workings.

DERBY Turning
from Douglas Street
into Osmaston Road
on route 33 is No
219 (DRC 219),
one of a batch of 20
Willowbrook-bodied
Sunbeam F4s that
were new between
November 1952 and
March 1953; No 219
would be sold for scrap
in February 1967.

DERBY The last new trolleybuses for the Derby
system were delivered between February 1960
and May 1960; numbered 236 to 243 (SCH 236 to
243), they were Roe-bodied Sunbeam F4As. This
is No 241 (SCH 241) overtaking tower wagon
No 4 (ARC 267) on Osmaston Road overbridge
near Litchurch Lane. The tower wagon was a Tilling
Stevens B20 chassis that had been a searchlight unit
owned by the War Department until purchased
by Derby from Salford Corporation on 31 March
1947; the combined chassis and tower was first
licensed on 7 June 1948, and the wagon was sold
for scrap in February 1967.

Left: **NOTTINGHAM** The Nottingham photographs were taken on the following day, 8 August. Between March and August 1945 Nottingham took delivery of ten Karrier Ws, Nos 459 to 465 with Roe bodywork and Nos 466 to 468 with Brush bodywork. By the time this view was taken only two of the ten, Nos 460 and 461 (GTV 660 and GTV 661), survived. Carrying out learner duties at the Nuttall Road, Cinderhill, terminus is No 460; it would be sold for scrap in June 1965.

Right: **NOTTINGHAM** A few minutes later, passing No 460 is Midland General No 452 (971 ARA), an ECW-bodied Bristol LD6G new in August 1956, working route C5 from Alfreton to Nottingham via Jacksdale.

1963 Arrivals & Departures

NOTTINGHAM Working service 40 outside the Central Market in King Edward Street is No 461 (GTV 661), the other surviving Roe-bodied Karrier W from the 1945 batch. All ten were delivered with wooden slatted seats, but these were replaced by upholstered seats in 1949. No 661 was sold for scrap in June 1965.

Births

James May	Journalist	16 January
Ian Cook	Footballer	18 January
Andrew Ridgely	Musician	26 January
George Monbiot	Journalist	27 January
Martin Bashir	Journalist	29 January
Jerome Flynn	Actor	16 March
David Thewlis	Actor	20 March
Julian Lennon	Musician	8 April
Natasha Richardson	Actress	11 May
Jason Isaacs	Actor	6 June
George Michael	Musician	25 June
Tracey Emin	Artist	3 July
Fatboy Slim (Norman Cook)	Musician	31 July
Tamsin Archer	Musician	3 August
Jarvis Cocker	Musician	19 September
Rick Allen	Musician	1 November
Lena Zavaroni (d.1999)	Musician	4 November
Nicolette Sheridan	Actress	21 November
Eddie 'The Eagle' Edwards	Ski-Jumper	5 December

Deaths

Edward Titchmarsh	Mathematician	(b.1899)	18 January
Hugh Gaitskell	Politician	(b.1906)	18 January
J. C. Powys	Writer	(b.1872)	17 June
Guy Burgess	Double agent	(b.1911)	30 August
Peter Craven	Motorcycle racer	(b.1934)	20 September
Aldous Huxley	Writer	(b.1894)	22 November
C. S. Lewis	Writer	(b.1898)	22 November
John F. Kennedy	US President	(b.1917)	22 November

Above: **NOTTINGHAM** In Lower Parliament Street by the King Edward Street junction and passing the Palais de Danse on the right is No 469 (HAU 169), a Park Royal-bodied Karrier W new in March 1946; it would be withdrawn and sold in July 1965. The Palais de Danse, built by Midland Palais de Danse Limited, opened on the corner of King Edward Street, John Street and Convent Street (now Upper Parliament Street) on 24 April 1925 and was originally designed as a dance hall and billiard saloon. The dance hall was considered to be one of the finest of its kind outside London and its exterior architectural features were distinctive, particularly the large ornate globe. The Palais could accommodate 1,000 dancers comfortably and dancing would take on most evenings at 8.00pm.

Above right: **NOTTINGHAM** Heading for the depot in Long Row at Market Square is No 471 (HAU 171), another of the batch of ten Park Royal-bodied Karrier Ws new in February to April 1946. This trolleybus would be one of the three that remained in service in 1965.

Right: **NOTTINGHAM** Crossing the railway and canal bridge on Wilford Road is No 486 (KTV 486), a Roe-bodied BUT 9611T new in October 1948 and sold for scrap in May 1965. Note the British Waterways warehouse in the background, which was built in the 1930s of reinforced concrete and considered at the time to be the best of its type in the country. It is now a Grade II-listed building and has been recently restored, currently serving as luxury apartments.

Above: **NOTTINGHAM** On learner duties at the junction of Nuttall Road and Bells Lane, the Cinderhill terminus, is No 487 (KTV 487) of the same batch. In the opposite direction, working Midland General route B4 between South Normanton and Nottingham, is an ECW-bodied Bristol LD6G.

Right: **NOTTINGHAM** trolleybus route 39 ran from Carlton Post Office Square to Wollaton Park, and operated until 30 September 1965. Picking up passengers at a very busy Carlton terminus is No 516 (KTV 516), a Brush-bodied BUT 9641T new in March 1950. It was withdrawn when trolleybus operations finished at the end of June 1966.

Left: **CARDIFF** was quite late in introducing trolleybuses, the first examples not taking to the streets until 1 March 1942. The intention had been to replace the city's remaining trams with trolleybuses in 1939, but the outbreak of war delayed matters. However, the trolleybus system expanded until the last extension (to Ely) was inaugurated in May 1955, taking the trolleybus fleet to 79 vehicles. This is No 209 (CKG 199), an NCME-bodied AEC 664T one of the first batch of trolleybuses. This view was taken on 9 May at the junction of Newport Road and City Road, and No 209 was sold for scrap soon afterwards.

The Beatles album Please Please Me *topped the album charts from 5 May 1963 for 30 weeks, being replaced by the next Beatles album,* With the Beatles.

Above: **CARDIFF** Arriving at Roath Road depot on 8 May is No 210 (CKG 200), the last numerically of the 1942 NCME-bodied AEC 664Ts. Passing is No 129 (DUH 316), a Bruce-bodied Bristol KW5G new in 1949, which was sold for scrap in June 1965.

Left: **CARDIFF** A few minutes after the photograph on the front cover was taken, with Clarence Bridge now clear of obstruction, this is No 266 (FBO 86), a Bruce/East Lancashire vehicle new in 1950 and sold for scrap in 1966. The bridge was opened by the Duke of Clarence on 17 September 1889.

CARDIFF Nos 211 to 230, East Lancashire-bodied BUT 9641Ts new in 1948, were the first of an order for 70 double-deck trolleybuses based on the wartime design. All of Cardiff's post-war trolleybuses were 8 feet wide and operated a pay-as-you-enter system using the rear for entrance and the front air-operated sliding door for exit. However, problems with the latter led to them being sealed in 1954 and subsequently panelled over. This view of No 212 (DBO 472) shows the neat work in panelling over the front door.

PONTYPRIDD The last day of trolleybuses in Pontypridd was 31 January 1957, but some remnants of the system were still visible in May 1963, such as this traction standard with bracket arm. The bus, No 75 (VNY 653), is one of six Roe-bodied Guy Arab IVs that were purchased new as trolleybus replacements in 1957.

Ipswích

Top left: IPSWICH Inbound to Electric House in Landseer Road at the Gainsboro terminus at its junction with Clapgate Lane on 31 January is No 116 (ADX 186); a Park Royal-bodied Sunbeam F4, it entered service on 1 June 1950, was withdrawn on 28 February 1963 and sold for scrap on 23 April.

The No 1 single on this day was Diamonds by Jet Harris and Tony Meehan, both former members of The Shadows.

Bottom left: IPSWICH Leaving Clapgate Lane into Nacton Road on 31 January is No 29 (GPV 29), one of six Park Royal-bodied AEC Regent Vs delivered during the first two weeks of 1958.

Readíng

READING At the original Northumberland Avenue terminus on a wintry 3 January is No 172 (ERD 143), one of a batch of 12 Park Royal-bodied Sunbeam S7s that entered service in November 1950. No 172 was part of the fleet of trolleybuses that were withdrawn at the end of the Reading system on 3 November 1968.

On this day conditions in the UK led to the cancellation of all but three of the scheduled third round matches of the 1962-63 FA Cup. The blizzard was the worst snow in Britain's 100 years of recorded weather history.

READING At the new Northumberland Avenue terminus on 20 January is No 173 (ERD 144) of the same batch.

Three days after this view was taken, British MI5 agent Kim Philby, who was secretly working as a double agent for the Soviet Union's NKVD, disappeared after having a drink with a colleague in Beirut. Five months later, on 30 July, the Soviet Union announced that he had been given asylum there and confirmed his identity as a Soviet spy.

Above left: **READING** At the junction of Blagdon Road and Northumberland Avenue on 10 January, struggling to cope with the treacherous conditions is No 177, another of the Park Royal-bodied Sunbeam S7s, this one new in December 1950. This trolleybus had received an extensive body overhaul in 1960.

Above: **READING** At St Mary's Butts terminus, also on 10 January, is No 180 (ERD 151), a Park Royal-bodied Sunbeam S7 that was withdrawn and sold for scrap in January 1968. Many monuments were raised around Britain to celebrate Queen Victoria's Golden Jubilee; the fountain seen here in St Mary's Butts was used to water horses.

Left: **READING** The snow became worse on that January day, and No 180 is seen again, showing an incorrect destination display, sliding on a treacherous Buckland Road while heading for Northumberland Avenue.

Above: **READING** In service to Tilehurst on 31 March on Kings Road at its junction with Kennet Street is No 189 (VRD 189), a Burlingham-bodied Sunbeam F4A that was new in August 1961 and sold for scrap in March 1969. The trolleybus alongside, being towed, is South Shields No 204 (CU 3593), a Weymann-bodied Karrier E4 nearing the end of its journey for preservation by Reading Transport Society.

On this day the 1962 New York City newspaper strike ended after 114 days.

Above right: **SLOUGH** South Shields No 204 is seen again on the same day at Slough railway station, being passing by Thames Valley No 732 (JRX 807), an ECW-bodied Bristol KSW6B new in 1954.

Right: **SLOUGH** A few minutes later, entering Slough station while heading for Maidenhead, is Thames Valley No 877 (545 BBL), an ECW-bodied Bristol FLF6G that was just two months old when photographed.

Right: **READING** It is 17 November and arriving at Mill Lane for preservation is Bournemouth No 212 (ALJ 973), a Park Royal-bodied Sunbeam MS2 that was delivered on 4 March 1935 and entered service on the 25th. It was purchased by Reading Transport Society for £67, including towing costs. Doing the towing is FRU 180, a Guy Arab breakdown lorry that had been converted from bus No 44 in June 1961 and is carrying trade licence plate 094 EL.

Main picture: **READING** On tow to Chadwell Heath, near Romford, for preservation with the Reading Transport Society on 19 May is Cardiff No 203 (CKG 193), an NCME-bodied AEC 664T new in 1942; it returned to Reading in 1964. Travelling in the opposite direction, working route 36 to Cadmore End, is Thames Valley No 626 (GJB 264), an ECW-bodied Bristol LWL6B new in 1952.

Above: **MAIDSTONE** Departing from Loose terminus for Barming on 7 February is Maidstone No 55 (GKN 380), a Sunbeam W4; new in June 1943 with a Park Royal body, it was rebodied by Roe in September 1960. The Maidstone trolleybus system was abandoned on 15 April 1967, and No 55 was sold for scrap at that time.

Left: **MAIDSTONE** At Park Wood at the end of the one-way system is No 54, also new in June 1943 with a Park Royal body and rebodied by Roe in October 1960. This trolleybus survived until the end of the system and was scrapped in August 1967.

Above: **MAIDSTONE** No 68 (HKR 7), an NCB-bodied Sunbeam W4 new in January 1947, has left Park Wood heading for Barming and is heeling over while negotiating the roundabout at 'The Wheatsheaf' inn. No 68 survived to the end of the system, being scrapped by August 1967.

Above right: **BOURNEMOUTH** The winter of 1962/63 was particularly hard and for the first time in its history Bournemouth's trolleybus service was completely shut down on 30 December 1962. On 17 January, with snow still evident, No 236 (KLJ 336), a Weymann-bodied BUT 9641T, is working route 31, Triangle to Columbia Road, at The Square. This trolleybus entered service on 1 October 1950, and was one of ten BUT 9641Ts that had their front staircase removed, although the front exit doors were retained, the work being completed on No 236 in December 1962. It was withdrawn in mid-April 1966 and sold for scrap for £75 to Wombwell Diesels in December 1966.

Right: **BOURNEMOUTH** Working route 25 to Westbourne on the same day is another of the same batch, No 240 (KLJ 340). Interestingly, this view was taken a month before the trolleybus had its front staircase removed, which increased the seating capacity to 68. Route 25's last day of service was Sunday 25 September 1966, and No 240 was withdrawn from service on that day and sold for scrap in December.

Right: **PORTSMOUTH**
Heading north at the junction of Northern Parade and London Road, Hilsea, working route 5 on 24 January, is No 301 (ERV 926), a Burlingham-bodied BUT 9611T new in 1950. It survived until the closure of the city's trolleybus system, the last day of operations being just six months away when this view was taken.

Far right:
PORTSMOUTH
Working route 6 is No 309 (ERV 934), a Burlingham-bodied BUT 9611T new in 1951. It is 24 January again, and the trolleybus is climbing up to Cosham railway bridge heading south along Northern Road; it was withdrawn from service on 27 June.

Right: **PORTSMOUTH**
Heading south along London Road, Hilsea, on the same day is No 311 (ERV 936) another of the same batch of BUT 9611Ts new in 1951. On the right is the completely frozen Ports Creek – the ice extended right out to the open sea.

PORTSMOUTH Working route 43A on 24 January, and also seen on London Road, Hilsea, is Southdown No 317 (JCD 17), one of a batch of 80 all-Leyland PD2/1s new in 1948; No 317 was new in February of that year, was withdrawn from service in 1965 and sold for scrap in August 1966. The Southdown depot is in the left distance.

Index of operators and vehicles

Aberdeen: BRS 253 6; DRG 451 5
Ashton trolleybuses: 83, 86 35
Bournemouth trolleybuses: 212 60; 236, 240 62
Bradford trolleybuses: 593 23; 726 24; 733 25; 743 26; 757, 811, 831 27; 832 28-29; 844 29
Cardiff trolleybuses: 203 60; 209, 210 54; 212 55; 266 54
Derby trolleybuses: 171, 172, 206 48; 219, 241 49; tower wagon ARC 267 49
Doncaster buses: 172 GDT 18; 4166 DT 20; 4167 DT 21; trolleybuses: 369 18; 373 19, 20; 375 21, 22
Dundee: ATS 901 7
Huddersfield trolleybuses: 569 29-30; 622 31
Hull trolleybuses: 110 15, 16; 111 17
Ian Glass: SS 7501 8
Ipswich: ADX 186, GPV 29 56
Maidstone trolleybuses: 54, 55 61; 68 62
Manchester buses: GVR 144 33; UNB 578 32; trolleybuses: 1308 35; 1310 32; 1316, 1320, 1331 33; 1357 34; 1361 35
McGill: CHS 355, GVD 47, JXC 201 8
McLachlan: SB 7600 7

Middlesbrough trolleybuses: 2 13; 6 14
Midland General: 971 ARA 50
Newcastle-upon-Tyne trolleybuses: 488 10, 11; 523 11
Nottingham trolleybuses: 460 50; 461 50; 469, 471, 486 52; 487, 516 53
Pontypridd: VNY 653 55
Portsmouth buses: JCD 17 64; trolleybuses: 301, 309, 311 63
Reading trolleybuses: 172 56; 173 57; 177, 180 58; 189 59
SMT: NSG 779 8
South Shields trolleybuses: 204 59; 254, 267, 270 12; 206, 246 13
Sutherland Transport and Trading: FJS 685 4
Thames Valley: 545 BBL 59; GJB 264 60
Walsall trolleybuses: 304 41; 305, 334 42; 354 46; 640, 854 42; 856 1, 43; 862 44; 864, 865 45; 866 46; 869 47; 870 47; 872, 874 43; 877 44
Western SMT: JSD 905 9; BCS 301, BCS 302 9
Wolverhampton buses: FJW 550 37; trolleybuses: 402, 404 40, 414 36; 432 37; 435 36; 463, 470, 486 40; 499 47; 621, 626, 635 38; 638 39